smALL FOR THE GLORY OF GOD

Saint John the Dwarf

By Susan Peek

Illustrated by Martina Parnelli

Seven Swords Publications
ISBN: 0-9970005-4-6
ISBN-13: 978-0-9970005-4-2

Artwork © Jean Kenney

Cover Design: Theresa Linden

For ordering information, please contact:
SevenSwordsPublications@gmail.com

www.susanpeekauthor.com

When our loving Father in Heaven created us, He made us all different from each other. Some people have brown hair, while others have black, or red, or blond. Some folks need glasses in order to see, while others have excellent eyesight but can't walk without crutches. There are fair-skinned people and dark-skinned people, and no one in the world is exactly the same as anyone else.

But sometimes, when God creates a beautiful new baby, He decides to make it even *more* different than others. He makes this little boy or girl special -- *extra, extra special* -- so that on earth things may be a lot harder for that person, but in Heaven a wonderful reward will be waiting. God does this for a reason -- a great secret reason which nobody quite understands. But how happy those special children of His will be in eternity when they find out why they were chosen and not someone else instead.

This story is about a little boy like that . . .

This little boy's name was John, and he lived in Egypt over sixteen hundred years ago (which is a long, *long* time ago). When he was born, his parents discovered that John was different from other children in this *extra special* way. For their baby boy was a dwarf! That meant he would never ever grow tall. He would stay very small even when he was a grown-up man.

Little John had much to suffer. He couldn't do the type of things that other children do easily without even thinking about. For example, John couldn't reach things on high shelves, or open door handles, unless he first dragged over a chair and climbed on it. Sometimes mean children in the village would stare at him and laugh, and this made him feel sad. He had pain in his legs and back, and he seemed to get tired quickly. He couldn't always play the fun games that his big brother Daniel did. There were lots of hard things like this which happened to John every day, and all because he was short when everyone else was tall.

If Little John had wanted to, he could easily have become angry or upset about all this and gone around moping and feeling sorry for himself. Sometimes he must have wanted so badly to be tall like everyone else, and surely there were days when he couldn't hold back his tears at the cruel teasing of the village bullies.

But Little John had a secret in his heart.

The secret was that he loved God very much, and he wanted to become a saint. Not just a pretend saint, but a *real* saint. In order to do this, he realized he was going to have to be brave. Very brave. He was going to have to do *all* for the glory of God, even if it meant staying *small* for the glory of God!

So he held on tightly to his secret, and offered up all his sorrows and disappointments and pain to Our dear Lord with a big smile, even when he felt sad inside. It wasn't easy, of course. It isn't easy for any of us. But then John began looking at his Crucifix every day and something amazing started to happen. The more he looked at Jesus on the Cross, the more he felt his heart growing. His body stayed small, but his heart was becoming *huge* with love, and it was such a wonderful, happy feeling that all John wanted to do was look at his Crucifix more and more! (He didn't know it, of course, but his secret was starting to come true . . .)

Now one day, when John was eighteen years old, a holy hermit came down from the distant hills and preached to the townsfolk. (A hermit is like a monk who lives alone in a cave.) The hermit was Saint Poemen, and when John heard his beautiful sermon he decided that he, too, wanted to live that way and become a holy hermit himself.

So a few days later, John packed a bag with a loaf of bread and a blanket, said good-bye to his parents and his brother Daniel (whom he knew he was going to miss really bad), and hiked all the way to the cave in the wilderness where Saint Poemen lived.

"I want to be a hermit too," he announced when he reached the saint's dwelling. "Please let me live here with you."

At first Saint Poemen thought that his rough way of living would be much too hard for such a small dwarf. He gently told John to go home. But, because it was late at night by now and already dark, he agreed to let John stay with him until morning.

John felt very let down as he unrolled his blanket and got ready to go to sleep, but he tried not to show it. He looked at his Crucifix (which he had taken with his blanket and his loaf of bread) and offered up this great disappointment to Jesus with a courageous smile.

But in the middle of the night a wonderful thing happened. An Angel woke Saint Poemen up and said, "God wants Little John to live in the cave next door to yours. It will be your special job to teach him to become a saint!"

When morning came, Saint Poemen told John that he could stay. But he didn't say anything yet about his visitor from Heaven during the night. Instead, he simply asked John to fast with him for the next few days. (To fast means not to eat anything, or at least not eat much.) The reason Saint Poemen asked this was because he wanted to make sure the Angel he had seen was a real one, and not just something he had dreamed about.

So, for three whole days neither of them ate any food at all. You can imagine how hungry they must have become! John's stomach kept growling and growling, but his heart was full of hope. Maybe the holy hermit would let him stay after all! They both prayed as hard as they could to know God's will.

Then, on the third day, the Angel came back! This time John saw him too. The heavenly spirit had brought something with him -- it was a miniature monk's habit made of rough wool, and just the perfect size for a dwarf! The Angel blessed it for John to put on. Now John was an official hermit! He excitedly moved his blanket and uneaten loaf of bread into the cave next door and set up house.

Saint Poemen was glad too, and started right away to teach his eager young student. The first lesson was going to be on Perfect Obedience, because no monk can be holy without knowing *that*! So Saint Poemen took a dead stick and pushed it into the ground. "Water this every day," he told John with a secret smile.

Now everybody knows that a dead stick can't grow! That would be silly. John was a bit confused, but he obeyed his teacher anyhow. The nearest water was several miles away, which for anyone is a fair distance. But for a dwarf, it's a very long walk indeed! Yet Little John didn't complain. He cheerfully took a bucket every morning and set off on his journey to the river. He had to stop many times on the way, because his legs got very tired, but he never gave up.

John watered the dead stick each day for three entire years. Imagine that! Then, a miracle happened. The stick suddenly blossomed! Beautiful flowers appeared on its spindly branches, then the flowers turned into fruit. Saint Poemen was just as excited as John was, and very pleased with him for having obeyed so perfectly. He took the delicious harvest to other hermits nearby and told them, "Take and eat the fruit of Obedience!"

After that, John became holier every day, in huge leaps and bounds. His secret was coming true! He became *so holy*, in fact, that when Saint Poemen died, other men came to John and asked *him* to be *their* teacher! One of them was a huge giant who had once been a bandit and a murderer, but gave up his sins and learned to love God. He became a saint too -- Saint Moses the Black. (Saint Moses has a whole story to himself, but that's another book . . .)

Even John's own big brother Daniel showed up one day asking to be a hermit. John was so excited to see his brother again and welcomed him with joy.

Normally, a dwarf is not allowed to become a priest. But when the Bishop saw how holy John was, he decided to make an exception and ordained him. John is the only dwarf in all of history who was able to become a priest. Now he could hold Jesus in his hands and offer Him to God the Father in the Holy Mass. John had never been so happy in his life and was always grateful for such a special privilege from God!

The little priest loved Our Lord so much that he thought about Him all the time. Sometimes this caused embarrassing problems. John's mind was so busy thinking about God all the time that he would forget everything else.

Once, a man came up the hillside on a camel. He knocked on John's cave-door and asked if he could please borrow some tools to make something . . .

"Of course," John answered, always happy to help. "I'll fetch them right away." He headed back into his cave to get them. But somewhere between the doorway and the corner where he kept his tools, John got all distracted thinking about God. He completely forgot about the man on the camel and fell on his knees to pray instead!

The man outside waited for a polite few minutes, then knocked again. A second time, John came to greet him. "The tools," the man reminded him. "May I borrow them please?"

"Oh yes," John answered, a little embarrassed. "I forgot." So back he went into his cave. But the same thing happened. He started thinking about God, and the tools vanished right out of his mind.

By now the man on the camel was getting impatient. He knocked for the third time. Again, John got up from his knees and went to the door. He was starting to feel bad for making the poor man wait so long, but truly, he just couldn't stop himself from praying!

"I'm sorry," the little dwarf apologized. "I promise I won't forget again."

So this time he went back into the cave repeating to himself over and over again the words, "The camel, the tools. The camel, the tools." And that's how he finally remembered what to do!

Another time, a hermit-friend of his came to visit. John started talking about God's great love and how beautiful Heaven was going to be. He got so excited about such a wonderful subject that he talked on and on, all day and all night, without even stopping to eat! (If only we could all get that excited about Heaven. Wouldn't that be wonderful?)

Years passed. John was growing older. He spent his days praying and writing about God. Even to this day, monks still read the holy books he wrote.

Then one day, some awful news reached the area where all the hermits lived. A tribe of horrible barbarians called Berbers were heading their way. Now these Berbers were really scary warriors. They were attacking the nearby villages and killing the people. Everyone was terrified and trying to run away. John and the other monks would have to flee if they wanted to stay alive!

Some of the hermits were very frightened. But John was not even scared at all. He knew God was their Father and would take perfect care of them. He comforted the other monks and calmly led them away from their beloved caves in the wilderness.

The group traveled a long distance, and crossed a huge river called the Nile. They had many exciting adventures on the way, but at last they settled in a new place where they would be safe from the Berbers.

It was here in a new cave that John spent his last years on earth. He died as an old man in his seventies.

At the moment of his death, one of his friends saw the dwarf's pure-white soul being carried to Heaven by angels.

Little John's body was always very small, but his love for God was enormous, and he is truly a giant among God's special ones. From Heaven he loves and protects everyone who prays to him, but he takes extra delight in helping children who are different, like him.

His Feast Day is October 17, and every year on that day, there is a big party in Heaven for Little Saint John the Dwarf.

The End

About the Author

Susan Peek is a wife, mother, Third Order Franciscan, creative writing teacher and best-selling Catholic novelist. Her passion is writing stories of little-known saints and heroes. She is an active member of the Catholic Writers' Guild and one of the founding members of Catholic Teen Books.

All of her young adult novels have been awarded the coveted Catholic Writers' Guild Seal of Approval and are implemented into Catholic school curricula not only across the nation, but in Canada, Australia, and New Zealand as well. "Saint Magnus, The Last Viking" and "The King's Prey" were both Amazon #1 Sellers among Catholic books. "The King's Prey" was also voted one of Catholic Reads TOP 10 BEST CATHOLIC BOOKS OF 2017 and was a Finalist for the 2018 Catholic Arts and Letters Award.
"Crusader King" was featured as one of the 50 Most Popular Catholic Home - schooling Books in 2013.

Susan lives in northeastern Kansas, where she is busy working on her new novel.

About the Illustrator

Artist, poet and writer Martina Parnelli resides in western Michigan where she enjoys learning about the local flora and teaching the chickadees to eat from her hand. She takes an interest in matters historical and astronomical as well as those relating to home crafts.

Her books for children are the *Little Runty Series* and *Fat John, His Little Lamb, and the Two Wise Owls* co-authored with Roberto Angelorum and published by Leonine Publishers. For teens and adults, she written plays including *Who Shall Wear the Wedding Veil?* and *Love's Labour Started.*

Exciting Fast-paced Saint Stories!

God's Forgotten Friends:
Lives of Little-known Saints

. . . Because the saints
weren't boring,
and neither should
their stories be!

www.susanpeekauthor.com

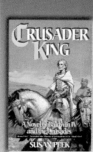

Martina Parnelli invites you to

Discover the adventures of Little Runty in these exciting

accounts taken from the *Mystical City of God:*

Did you know that reviews sell books?

If you have enjoyed this story, or other books by Susan Peek or Martina Parnelli,

please consider posting a brief review on Amazon, Goodreads, or your favorite book site.

Even a sentence or two would make the authors so happy!

Thank you and God bless!

Made in the USA
Columbia, SC
30 April 2019